Healthy Kids

With a foreword by Melinda French Gates

Maya Ajmera • Victoria Dunning • Cynthia Pon

Samoa

Charlesbridge

Zambia

All children, regardless of where they live, should have the opportunity to grow up healthy and lead a productive life. As a mother I feel fortunate to live in a place where my children and most other children are healthy because they have access to things like clean water, nutritious food, and vaccines.

In many other parts of the world, children are not so lucky. In my travels over the last decade to Africa and South Asia, I have met many women who must walk for hours just to fill a jug with clean water or get their children immunized at a local health clinic. Every day, mothers give birth to children who—especially in the early years of life—are at risk of getting very sick from pneumonia, meningitis, malaria, and many other diseases. Over seven million children die each year before they reach their fifth birthday. As my father-in-law, Bill Gates Sr., says, these are not just numbers, these are our neighbors.

The good news is that the world is making progress. There are millions of healthy kids alive today because of advances such as vaccines, better bed nets to protect against mosquitoes, and improved nutrition and medical care for mothers and their babies.

As you read this book, think of the millions of children who are fighting every day to survive. But also think of the millions of children who are thriving today because of the great progress that the world has made. We have the tools. We know they work. We owe it to all the children of the world to do all we can to give them the best chance to survive and succeed in life.

After all, these are our neighbors.

Melinda French Gates

Co-chair and trustee, Bill & Melinda Gates Foundation

Argentina

Healthy kids grow up strong, active, and ready to go!

Bhutan

Canada

Guatemala

Romania

Kenya

We eat nourishing food.

Vietnam

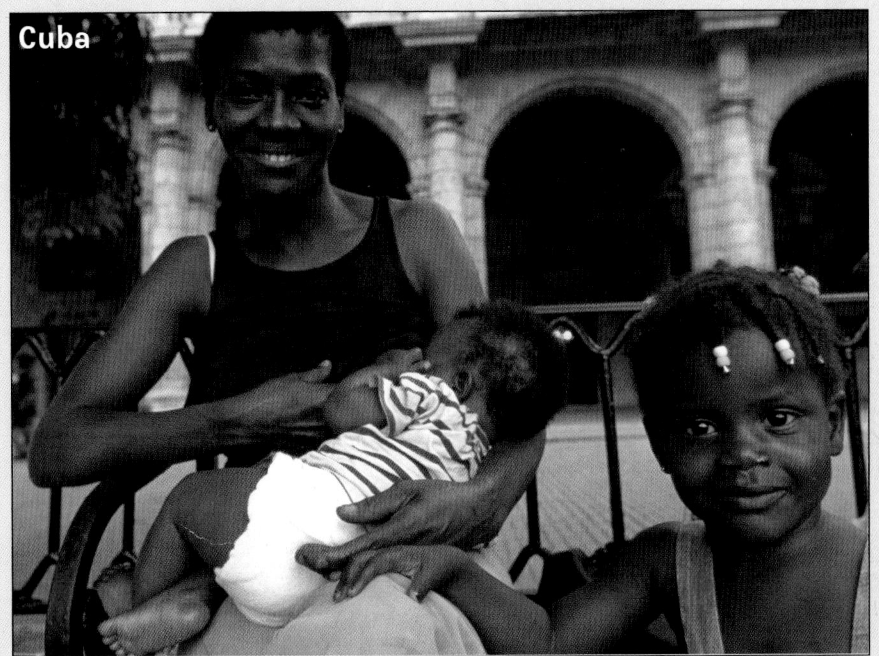

Sometimes we get a sweet treat!

Healthy kids need clean water to drink.

Japan

India

Ghana

Thailand

We scrub our hands with soap and water, wash our hair, and clean behind our ears, too.

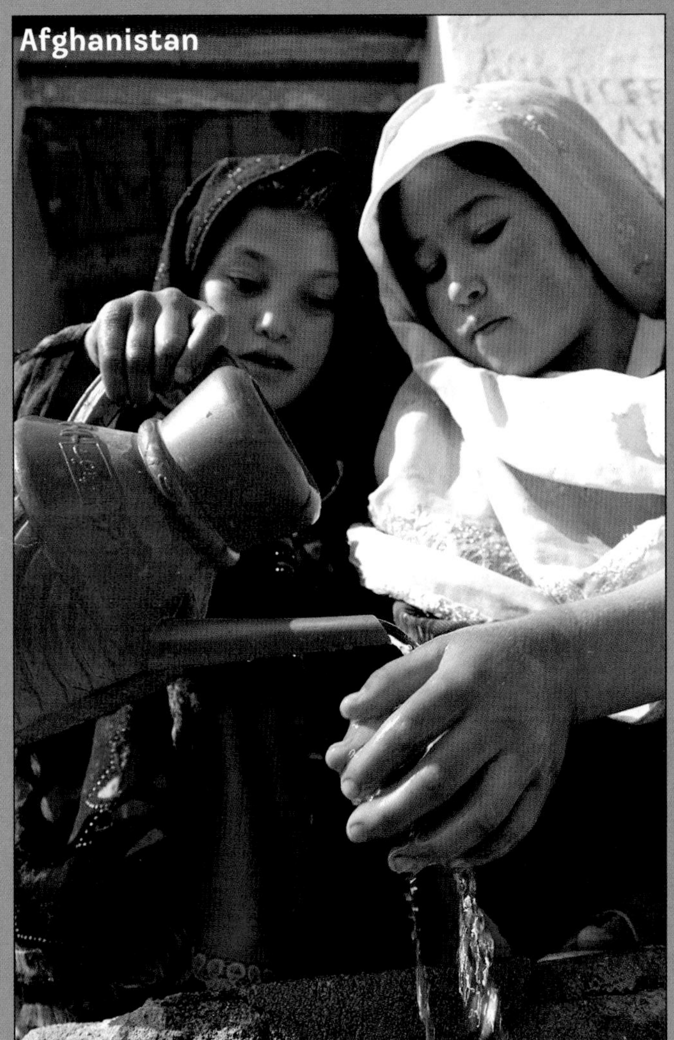
Afghanistan

USA

We use a toilet, a potty, a privy, a loo, a WC, an outhouse, or a pit latrine.

Guatemala

A safe, clean home protects us from the cold, wind, and rain.

China

Egypt

Suriname

A nurse or a doctor helps keep us healthy.

Uzbekistan

USA

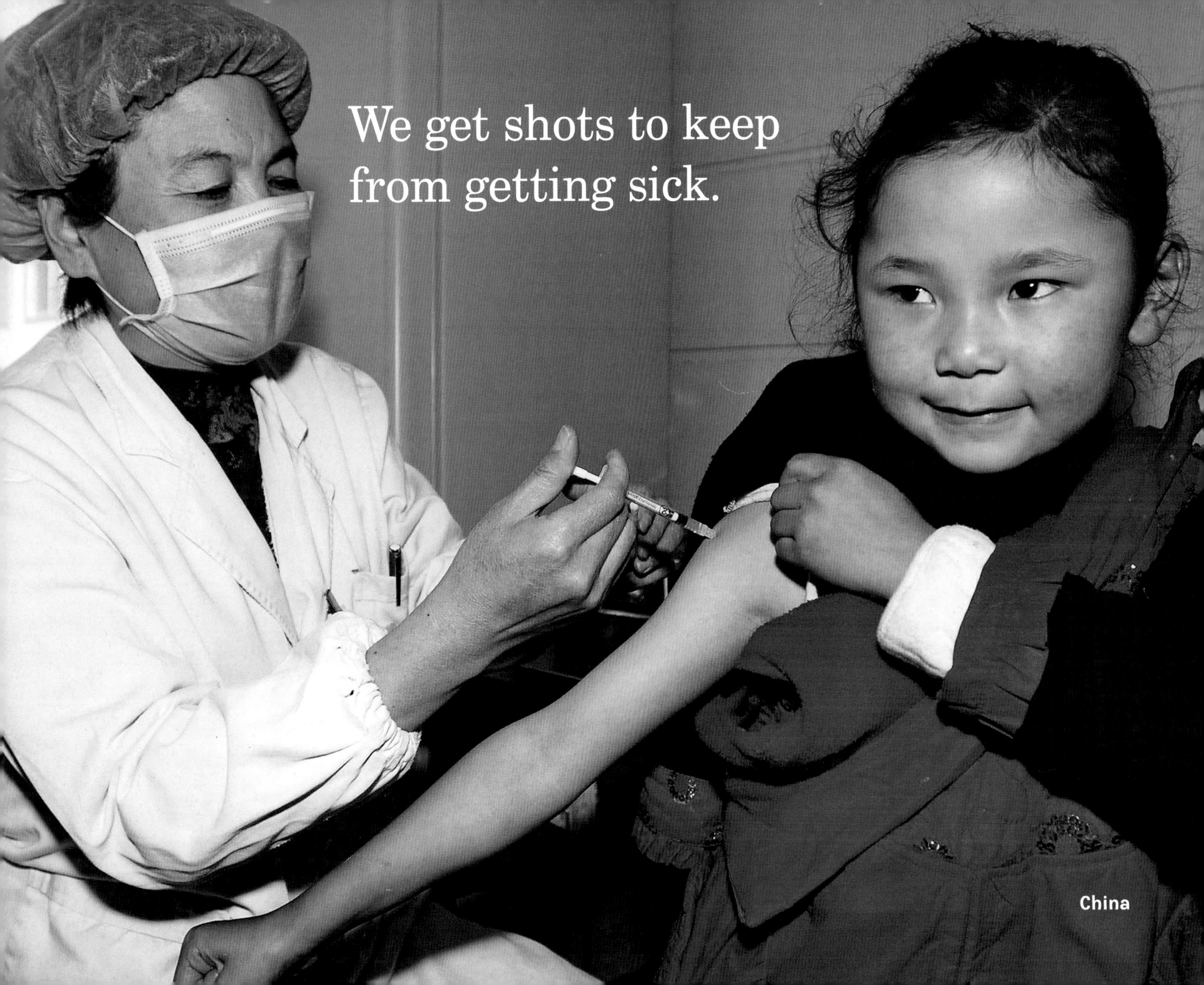
We get shots to keep from getting sick.

China

We brush our teeth after meals, and visit a dentist to keep our teeth strong.

Tonga

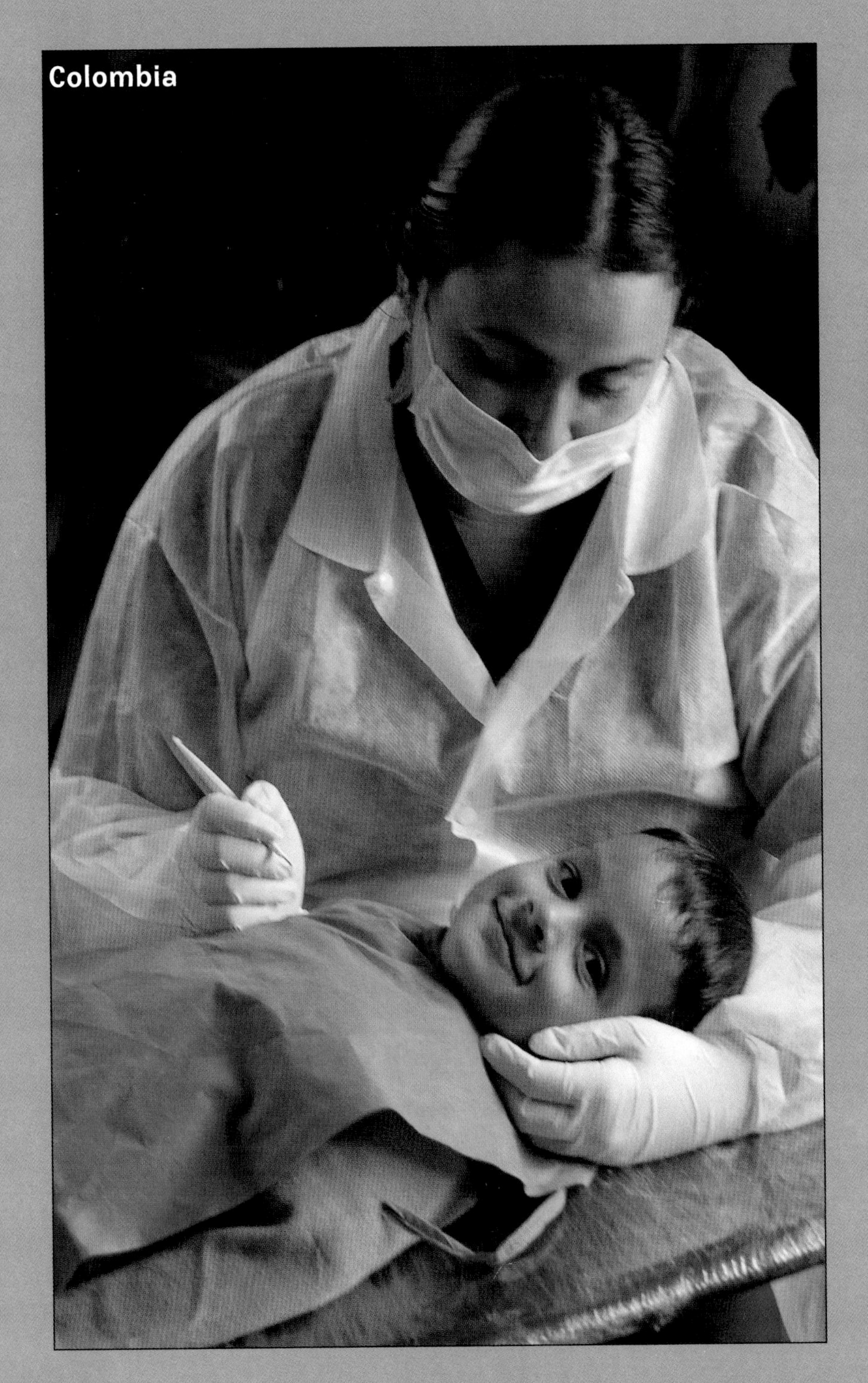

Look, no cavities!

We exercise and play all kinds of sports.

Australia

Mongolia

Greenland

We love to be outside!

We wear hats and shoes to protect us from the sun and rain.

Brazil

United Kingdom

Sometimes we sleep under nets that keep pesky mosquitoes away.

We wear seat belts on the road, and helmets when we bike or scoot.

Panama

USA

Botswana

We grow up surrounded by our families and communities, feeling safe and loved.

Syria

Bangladesh

We are healthy kids!

Healthy kids live all over the world.

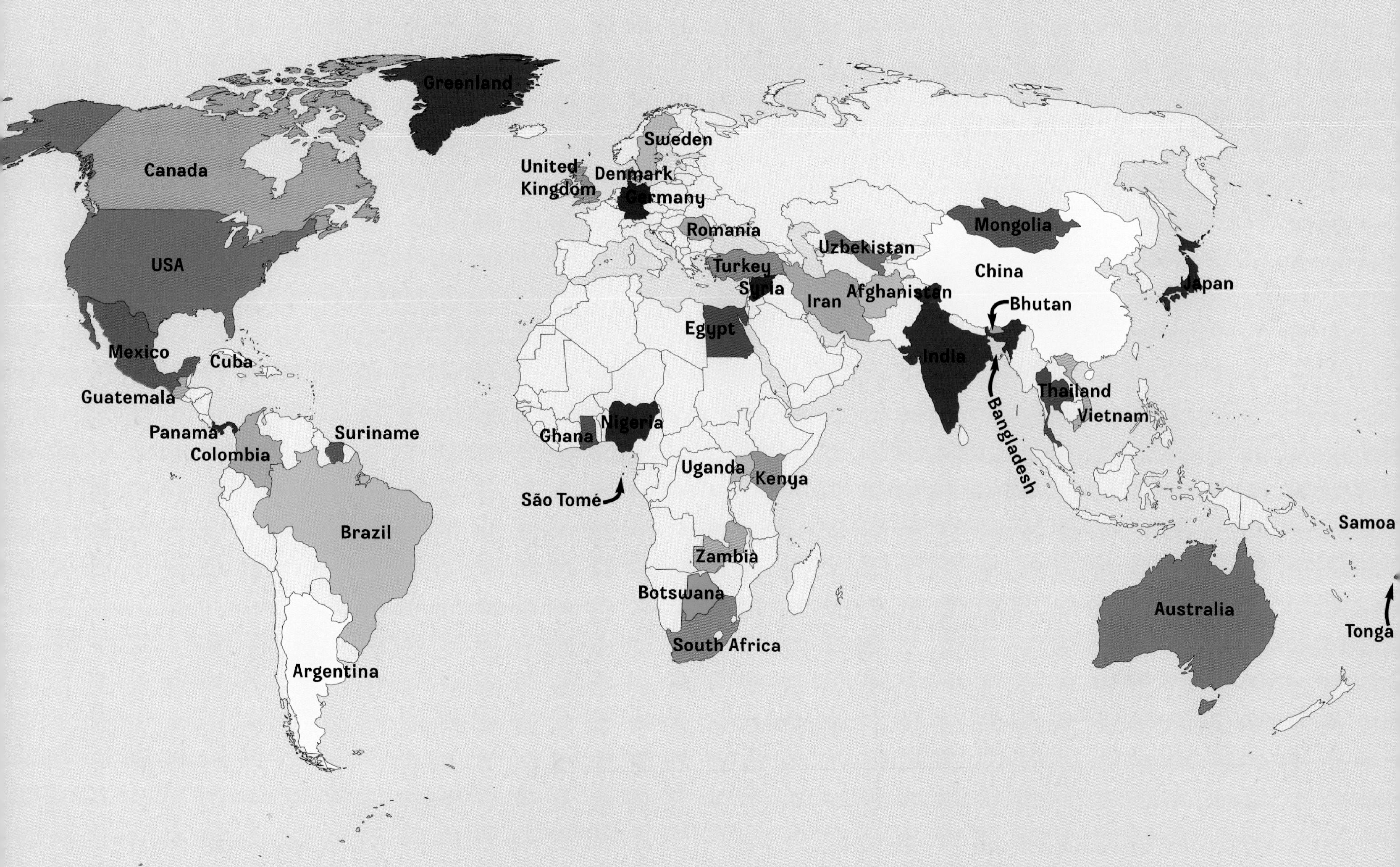

What Does It Take To Be a Healthy Kid?

Good Food and a Healthy Diet

Our bodies need fuel to run, jump, learn, and fight germs. Fruits, vegetables, and foods like milk, eggs, meat, nuts, and beans help our bones, brains, and muscles grow strong.

Eating a healthy diet is not always easy. If families don't have much money or if certain foods are in short supply, it can be tough to make healthy meals. One thing people do all over the world is plant gardens—and so can you! Even a small plot of land—in your yard, neighborhood, or at your school—can grow lots of yummy, nutritious food.

Clean Water for Drinking . . .

Did you know more than half of your body is made up of water? Healthy kids drink plenty of clean water, but in some places that may be hard to find. Dirty or contaminated water can make people very sick.

Kids in some communities help by collecting fresh rainwater and boiling or treating it so it is safe to drink. Water is heavy, but using a container shaped like a wheel makes moving it much easier. No matter where you live, you can conserve water by using only what you need.

. . . and for Washing

You also need clean water for washing your hands, especially after you use the bathroom and before you eat. Scrubbing with soap and clean water keeps diseases from spreading. If you sing the ABC song slowly while you wash, you'll be sure to scrub long enough to get rid of dirt and germs.

A Place to Use the Bathroom

Everybody pees and poops. But pee and poop, also called "waste," can spread diseases if they aren't handled properly.

South Africa

Pit latrines, septic tanks, and flush or composting toilets are all ways to treat or get rid of waste. Some groups help by building toilets in communities that need them. In some places, latrines are painted with colorful pictures, and kids learn about healthy bathroom habits from posters, plays, or even puppet shows!

A Safe, Clean Environment

Just like you, kids everywhere like to play with animals, dig up worms, wade in streams, and watch things grow. You need a clean world to explore, with fresh air to breathe. A healthy environment is free from trash, pollution, tobacco smoke, hazardous waste, and even dangers that can't be seen, like pesticides on plants and lead in paint.

We can all help make our environment healthy by keeping our communities litterfree, recycling, and protecting trees and vulnerable habitats.

Medical and Dental Care

No matter what you do to stay healthy, sometimes you still get sick. Taking medicine or seeing a nurse or doctor can help you get better. Scientists have also developed vaccines that help the body fight off diseases. Getting vaccine shots hurts for just a little bit, but they do their job well.

Healthy kids also keep their teeth clean and strong. You can protect your teeth by brushing after meals, flossing every day, and avoiding too many sweet treats and drinks. Getting check-ups with a dentist also helps keep smiles beautiful.

In some hard-to-reach places, help comes in different vehicles. Some kids visit the doctor or dentist on a dental bus, in an airplane set up for eyecare, or on board a medical ship!

Exercise

Hula hooping, climbing trees, playing tag—the list of fun exercises never ends. You don't need fancy equipment or lots of time to get fit. You can ride your bike to school, or take a walk

Iran

with your family. Your heart loves it when you exercise. Don't forget about exercising your mind, either. Being active gives your brain a boost so you'll find it easier to pay attention in school. Reading books or solving tricky puzzles gives you a mental workout, so you are ready for new challenges.

To Be Protected

Healthy kids are sheltered from heat, cold, rain, and snow. This means wearing the right clothes for the weather and protecting your skin from the sun. In some climates kids sleep under special nets that protect them from mosquitoes that carry a disease called malaria. It's also important for you and your family to practice safe habits such as wearing helmets on your bike and seatbelts in cars, and crossing the street only when you're sure it is safe.

Around the world, kids help keep other kids safe. They watch out for younger kids, help out as safety patrols around their schools, and work as lifeguards at swimming areas.

A Loving Family and Community

Feeling safe and loved is just as important as having a strong, healthy body. Your family and neighbors encourage you, watch out for you, and help you make good decisions. Lots of kids live with their grandparents and other family members, like aunts, uncles, and cousins. It's fun when there's always someone to play with!

Healthy kids have teachers who challenge them and help them grow. Many neighborhoods have clubs just for kids—places where you can play games and sports, learn a musical instrument, and explore your community.

What Else Can You Do?

Communities that have less money often find it harder to keep kids healthy. They usually have fewer hospitals or clinics for health care, or grocery stores where they can get good, fresh food. Some of these communities might be on the other side of the world, but others are close to home.

Helping all kids become healthy kids might seem like a big job, but there are lots of things you can do. You can organize a neighborhood clean-up day with your friends, or talk to your teachers about getting healthier food in the cafeteria. You can save your allowance or gift money and donate it to an organization working for better health around the world. Starting with little steps can lead to big changes.

So get out there and be a healthy kid!

São Tomé

To my niece, Ai-Li and my nephew, Rishi. May all children strive to be active and healthy—M. A.

To my amazing daughter, Grace, and the kids of our global neighborhood. May each and all enjoy good health—V. D.

To my niece, Alana, and nephew, Brennan. May all children laugh and grow strong—C. P.

Healthy Kids was developed by The Global Fund for Children (www.globalfundforchildren.org), a nonprofit organization committed to advancing the dignity of children and youth around the world. Global Fund for Children books teach young people to value diversity and help them become productive and caring citizens of the world.

With thanks to Elise Hofer Derstine, who coordinated the photo search, and to Kelly Swanson Turner, who assisted in drafting the backmatter.

Developed by The Global Fund for Children
1101 Fourteenth Street NW, Suite 420
Washington, DC 20005
(202) 331-9003
www.globalfundforchildren.org

Published by Charlesbridge
85 Main Street
Watertown, MA 02472
(617) 926-0329
www.charlesbridge.com

Part of the proceeds from this book's sales will be donated to The Global Fund for Children to support innovative community-based organizations that serve the world's most vulnerable children and youth. Details about the donation of royalties can be obtained by writing to Charlesbridge Publishing and The Global Fund for Children.

Library of Congress Cataloging-in-Publication Data
Ajmera, Maya.
Healthy kids / Maya Ajmera, Victoria Dunning, Cynthia Pon.
p. cm.
ISBN 978-1-58089-436-4 (reinforced for library use)
ISBN 978-1-58089-437-1 (softcover)
1. Children—Juvenile literature. 2. Children—Health and hygiene—Juvenile literature. 3. Multiculturalism—Juvenile literature. I. Victoria Dunning. II. Pon, Cynthia. III. Title.
HQ781.A26 2012
613'.0432—dc23 2012000784

Printed in Singapore

(hc) 10 9 8 7 6 5 4 3 2 1
(sc) 10 9 8 7 6 5 4 3 2 1

Display type set in Jesterday
Text type set in Century Schoolbook
Color separations by KHL Chroma Graphics, Singapore
Printed and bound September 2012 by Imago in Singapore
Production supervision by Brian G. Walker
Designed by Susan Mallory Sherman

Photo credits

Front Cover: © Alan Meier/Photolibrary.com
Back Cover: © Jesse Newman
p. 1: © Stephanie Rabemiafara/Art in All of Us.
p. 2: © Bill & Melinda Gates Foundation/Liz Gilbert.
p. 4: top left, © Jonathan Kim/Riser/Getty Images; bottom left, © Wolfgang Kaehler/Picade; bottom right, © Allen Donikowski/Flickr/Getty Images. **p. 5:** top left, © Jesse Newman; bottom left, © Russell Young/DanitaDelimont.com; right, © Duncan Maxwell/Robert Harding/Photolibrary.com. **p. 6:** © Jorgen Schytte/Photolibrary.com. **p. 7:** left, © Amer Ghazzal/Art Directors; top right, © Nick Servian/Picade; bottom right, © Westend61/Getty Images. **p. 8:** left, © Pholdar nine/a.collectionRF/Getty Images; right, © Doranne Jacobson.
p. 9: © Jorgen Schytte/Photolibrary.com.
p. 10: © Jesse Newman. **p. 11:** left, © Philippe Lissac/Godong/Photolibrary.com; right, © Shehzad Noorani/Agefotostock.com. **p. 12:** top left, © Sean Sprague/Agefotostock.com; bottom left, © Margaret Miller/Photo Researchers, Inc.; right, © Ulf Huett Nilsson/Johner Images/Getty Images. **p. 13:** © Anthony Asael/Art in All of Us. **p. 14:** left, © Bert Crawshaw/Art Directors; center, © Shehzad Noorani/Drik/Majority World/The Image Works. **p. 15:** © Doranne Jacobson.
p. 16: left, © Anthony Asael/Art in All of Us; right, © Frank Siteman/Science Faction/Getty Images.
p. 17: © sinopictures-ViewChin/ullstein bild/The Image Works. **p. 18:** © Spectrum Photofile. **p. 19:** left, © Shawn Malone/The Global Fund for Children; right, © Rune Johansen/Photolibrary.com. **p. 20:** left, © Chad Ehlers/Photolibrary.com; right, © Keren Su/DanitaDelimont.com.
p. 21: © B&C Alexander/ArcticPhoto.com.
p. 22: left, © Eye Ubiquitous/Photolibrary.com; right, © Helene Rogers/Art Directors. **p. 23:** © Irene Abdou/The Image Works. **p. 24:** © John Lund/Tiffany Schoepp/Blend Images/Getty Images. **p. 25:** left, © John & Lisa Merrill/DanitaDelimont.com; right, © Vincent Grafhorst/Afripics.com. **p. 26:** left, © Ali Kabas/DanitaDelimont.com; center, © Carole Al Farah/Majority World/The Image Works.
p. 27: © Sean Sprague/The Image Works. **p. 29:** © Pieter Hendrikse/Qdrum.co.za. **p. 30:** © Stephanie Rabemiafara/Art in All of Us. **p. 31:** © Anthony Asael/Art in All of Us.